SPANKY
AND HIS
GANG

A CORRECTIONAL OFFICER INSPIRES HOPE
THROUGH LOVE, LAUGHS AND COMPASSION

While every precaution has been taken in the preparation
of this book, the publisher assumes no responsibility for
errors or omissions, or for damages resulting from the use
of the information contained herein. In recounting the events
for this book, some details have been compressed, altered,
and omitted to better fit the narrative. Some of the dialogue
has been changed and/or abbreviated. Some of the names
of individuals have been changed.

SPANKY AND HIS GANG
A CORRECTIONAL OFFICER INSPIRES HOPE
THROUGH LOVE, LAUGHS AND COMPASSION

First edition. March 1, 2024.

Published by Big Kat Kreative LLC, 2024.
Printed in the United States of America.

Cover designed by Michael Mazewski of Big Kat Kreative

ISBN: 978-1-962796-01-9

Written by James Haas.

SPANKY
AND HIS
GANG

A CORRECTIONAL OFFICER INSPIRES HOPE
THROUGH LOVE, LAUGHS AND COMPASSION

JAMES HAAS

To Marcia,

For the mother of my kids, for the woman in my life for 57 years, for your fight with cancer, for your rides for Roswell. You are my rock star! I love you!

Me with my rock star!

"Life is about making a difference,
not just for oneself but for others."

– Lou Gehrig

Contents

Introduction

My name is James Haas and I retired after 34 years employed as a correctional officer at the Erie County Correctional Facility in Alden, New York. Over the years I jotted down notes from my experiences that filled a few steno pads with hopes I would one day share these stories with the world. Today is that day!

This book is told from my perspective and offers a firsthand look at what I observed and what I was directly involved in at the E.C.C.F., which I refer to as the prison. There were few dull days. It was a very interesting job and looking back I am proud of my career. I have several guards - as well as inmates -

who have become friends. They affectingly call me Spanky, my nickname that I picked up on the job.

It has always been my personal belief that you should treat others as you would like to be treated. I never imagined myself becoming a correctional officer. I took several civil service exams, scored a passing grade and was offered a position as a prison guard.

I am a happy person and a bit of a jokester who likes to see others smile. Given my nature, I always tried to make light of situations to keep the personalities of others relaxed. This approach often prevented things from becoming uncomfortable or moving in a negative direction.

All the inmates had a story to tell and I listened to each of them with compassion. I treated the inmates with dignity if they were respectful to me. I tried to show them a better way.

I let them know there is hope and a way toward a better future. Their prison sentence was not an end, but a transition toward a better life when they were discharged.

It is my sincere hope that I have touched many lives from the inmates to the guards with whom I worked. I always strived to leave everyone feeling a little bit better about themselves even in the tough conditions of prison life. I always wanted to put a smile on their faces.

I hope you enjoy reading my memories of life inside the prison walls.

With sincere gratitude,
Spanky

CHAPTER 1

Time For A Real Job

A lost soul in high school, college and in the job world, I was searching for direction.

I graduated and married Marcia, my high school sweetheart, at 19. We were young, but Marcia was the one thing in the world that I had no doubts about. Marcia was pregnant and we had a baby. We were instantly parents.

Now it was time for a real job.

I tried maybe 15 to 20 different jobs the first few years of marriage. I was taking exams for the city, county and state. I was hoping with a little bit of luck and a strong test score that I'd be able to get a really good job with benefits. And maybe even a retirement later in life.

Well, God was with me on the exam for Erie County Corrections. I passed and started on the job, September 4, 1972, at $6,800.00 a year.

Marcia saw my first check and said, "This is good for a week."

I said, "That's two week's pay."

She said, "We will starve to death!"

Well look at me all these years later, I don't look like I starved to death at 5 foot, 10 inches tall and 240 pounds. This was a good job that kept food on the table and made me feel good about myself.

The lost soul was found and I had a job that I enjoyed. I started my job at age 24 and said to myself, "What the hell do I actually do?"

I almost shit my pants on my first day. I was thinking about guarding 700 inmates and wasn't sure how I would be able to do this job. The first few weeks were very scary, and this was shortly after the Attica Riots, so that only heightened the anxiety. But we had to eat, we had bills to pay and I wanted to work, so I forged ahead.

CHAPTER 2

The Shit Jobs

I was trained by a dinosaur. This guy was a real old-time corrections officer. Most of the guards were 45 years or older. I was the baby of the group for a few years before the next guy was hired. Being the "new" guy, my job was every shit job in the place. They gave me two weeks training on every job and I kept detailed notes on 3x5 cards for each one.

My first shit job was just that.

I was running the kitchen when another old-timer named Tony, who had more hair on his ears than on his head and who looked about 10 years older than his 60-year-old self, came looking for me.

"Hey Haas!" Tony shouted as he entered the kitchen. "They want you in Segregation and I am here to relieve you."

So on to Segregation I go. I went down a long hallway. The place was like an old Humphrey Bogart movie with red waxed floors, brick walls and metal doors with bars.

I had to ring a bell to get in.

When the door opens I see a sergeant in a white shirt and about 10 correction officers in blue coats.

"Co-co-co-come on in here and pu-pu-put this ra-ra-ra-raincoat on," the sergeant said. "Everyone started smirking and grinning because the sergeant had a really bad stuttering problem, but sort of in a good way if you know what I mean.

"What do I need this raincoat for?" I asked.

"Ne-ne-never mind yo-yo-yo-you'll see" he replied as he opened the door to the Blue Room as his stuttering worsened in tense moments.

As I started to open the door something hit it, so I shut the door quickly. I looked at the sergeant and said, "Was that a ...?"

"You're fu-fu-fu-fucking right he is throwing sh-sh-shit balls," he replied. "Look at m-m-m-my sh-sh-shirt. He hit me with a shit ball."

He had a big spot on his white shirt the size of a baseball. Everyone laughed and I looked inside again

8

and there was shit all over. He even had a Nazi swastika on the wall made of shit.

What a foul smelling odor this created. It permeated the entire area. It was awful. Was this person nuts or what?

My job was to handcuff him and transport him to a hospital outside of the facility. He was mentally unstable and in need of professional help. He definitely needed medical attention.

I have a weak stomach and all the way to the hospital all I could smell was shit. I told the dinosaur, Norm, who was with me for the ride, that I could still smell shit.

He looked me up and down.

"If I were you," Norm said. "I would get a stick and poke the shit off your feet between the sole and heel of your shoes."

The inmate was seen by a doctor and the medical staff. Then we returned him to the facility.

CHAPTER 3

The Florida Kid

When working at the prison (the Erie County Corrections Facility), you always had inmates who were willing to do extra messy or dirty work for smokes or rewards.

One such inmate was Jimmy, better known as The Florida Kid. He was black and let's just say he was in touch with his feminine side. He became a person I could depend on when I needed help with prison chores or needed to get something cleaned.

When he mopped he was a dancing machine. He was a joy to watch. Always more water on the floor than in the bucket, but he made the mundane workday fun.

We worked together for more than 12 years as he was in and out for short bids over the years. He was the one who cleaned up the shit in the Blue Room.

Sadly, he was found dead in Buffalo in a cardboard shelter in a field during the winter.

He had sterno burns on his body trying to keep warm. With no friends, no relatives, no money, he was buried in a common grave.

I wish I could have said a prayer at his grave the day he was buried. We had a certain respect for each other that grew over the years. Unfortunately, I didn't know that he died until after the fact.

Even though I was a guard and Jimmy was an inmate, we had a high regard for one another on account of our working together. Everyone deserves to be treated with dignity. The Florida Kid didn't live a perfect life, but he was worthy of a better fate.

CHAPTER 4

The Third Shift

There are lots of memories from when I first worked the third shift at the facility, but this one particular night is a story in and of itself.

I was assigned to the Tailor Block on this night. It was dark on the block with only night lights to guide me. It was raining cats and dogs with loud thunder and lightning. The loud booms were the kind that caused dogs to hide.

The inmates were locked down so all I had to do was make my punches every half hour.

About three in the morning I could swear I heard people walking around outside their cells, but this was impossible. I moved on my tip toes so as not to wake any of the inmates. I was a little jumpy at each sound.

I was making my 3:30 a.m. punch when an inmate broke the silence and asked me if I could open a window. I almost jumped out of my skin at the sound of his voice, but played it cool and agreed to his request.

I had to push up and pull down on this large 1930s type window to open it. You had to hold it up when you hooked the top down by latching a chain to hold it down. And remember that it's still raining very hard at this point.

I walked away and he thanked me. About an hour later when I came back around he asked me to shut the window because he was cold.

I said sure, but little did I know the window had filled with water. So when I tipped the window down to close it, I got soaked. My shoes, my shirt and my pants were all drenched and about five inmates started laughing.

I took it in stride.

"You got me," I said. "But if you don't come out of your cell in the morning you'll know why."

That of course meant he would stay locked up, although it was just a joke he played on me. No harm done, so I didn't report him. It was just another lesson learned for the rookie, but I never opened a window like that again over the next 30 years.

CHAPTER 5

Firm But Fair Leadership

Mr. Albert J. Meyers was my first superintendent and was the guy that hired me. He called me to come in to be interviewed.

"So why do you want this job?" he asked. "So that you can wave a gun and badge at people"

"No sir," I replied. "I just want a good job with benefits because I have a family to take care of."

Well, lucky for me, he called me the next day and offered me the job.

What a break!

Everyone was afraid of A.J. Meyers. The inmates, the guards and just about everyone inside the walls of the prison. He treated us all alike, which is to say I believe he hated all of us.

That's how I remember him, but now looking back over the years he was the best boss that I ever worked for!

When he walked, he was the most erect man that I had ever seen. He was 72 years old and straight as an arrow. When he gave you his word, it was as good as gold.

It was rumored that when he worked at State Corrections that he had pulled the switch (old sparky) three times on the electric chair. He was a hard man to get close to, but he was fair with everyone.

He issued an order that no officers could use the phone unless approved by supervision. My first order to workover I got permission to call Marcia to let her know that I would be late. I was starting to call and as I got ready to talk I heard someone clear their throat and it was A.J. Meyers.

My eyes got big and I tried to talk but nothing came out.

"Officer Haas, do you have permission to use the phone?" said Meyers.

I replied in a very high-pitched woman's voice, "Yes SIR!"

He then smiled and walked away.

CHAPTER 6

No Pets, No Mop Strings, No Problem

We had a beautiful Deputy Superintendent Felix Mindy. He was Polish and had the driest sense of humor that I had ever seen.

I can remember he interviewed me for a rental of a county home near him. It was a house on the grounds of the old prison that was $62.50 a month to rent.

You normally had to have a lot of time on the job to get one of these homes. I only had about two years.

"Haas, how many kids do you have?" asked Mindy.

"Two girls," I replied.

"Do you have a pet?"

"No sir."

"Okay then, we will let you know in a few days."

Well, guess what. We got the house. What I didn't realize is that Mindy would be my neighbor.

Mindy came home one night and both my dogs (poodles) were outside. I got called down to his office the next day.

"Haas, I thought you said you didn't have a dog."

"I don't have a dog, I have two dogs."

"Go back to work and please keep those dogs quiet," he ordered me with a smirk on his face.

He was a very good boss and cared for the inmates. He would always help them as much as he could.

He wanted a clean place with good food and decent clothes for the inmates. He ran a good ship and wanted them to make it when they were released.

Mr. Mindy was a two-martini man. He would go to lunch and when he returned he was very loud about what needed to be done.

He would always tell the kitchen staff what he wanted done.

"Clean the mop strings from under the kitchen counters," instructed Mindy.

"Yes sir, Mister Mindy," was the consistent response from Officer Eddie, a.k.a. "Dirty Eddie," but he would never do it.

Eddie always laughed, looked at me and said, "Fuck those strings."

When Mindy retired he pulled Eddie aside.

"How do I argue with a guy who always agrees with me?" said Mindy. "But I want you to know that I knew you never cleaned those mop strings."

Mr. Mindy and his wife would babysit our daughters. Marcia just started working at Bells Supermarket in town. Mrs. Mindy called one day and asked if she could cook the frozen hot dogs for lunch. Marcia's answer was, "No. She likes them frozen."

Dawn, our oldest daughter, told her that she always eats them frozen like a Popsicle.

We laughed about that for years.

Is that child abuse?

Felix Mindy was a great boss and an even better neighbor.

CHAPTER 7

Sleigh Bells In The Night

While we were in bed trying to sleep on a hot summer night, I could hear bells ringing outside like Santa was coming.

Built in 1925, our county-owned home sat in the shadow of the prison, so the bells were an odd sound.

These row houses were built side-by-side in a group. Each one had a basement, a dining room, three bedrooms, a bathroom and a large walk-in attic. I went outside quickly to investigate and it turned out that it was a junkyard dog with sleigh bells sewn on his collar.

Standing there in just my underwear at 2:00 a.m., I called the dog up on our porch and cut the bells off.

The dog took off and I thought the problem was solved.

Not so. The next night the dog was back with sleigh bells on his collar.

On my way outside I grabbed a bar of soap. I tried to get him up on our porch but he started barking, so I threw the soap in the dark and hit him on the ass. He yelped and took off, bells ringing. It was one shot in a million. I went up to bed and told Marcia we'll never see him again.

Well that wasn't the end. The third night after a party-type night I was getting in bed later than usual and had just started to fall asleep and the bells started again.

I said to myself, "Not again."

So I am naked in bed, but hopped up and headed outside to get that damn dog. It's three o'clock and I'm looking for something to throw. I picked up my shoe as I went out on the back step. I saw the dog and threw my good shoe. I missed the dog and it went right through my neighbor's basement window, Mr. Mindy.

Luckily the screen held my shoe from falling into their basement. The dog took off never to be seen again but now I have to get my shoe.

I looked all around and thankfully did not see anyone because I am butt ass naked. Bare naked, not even any socks on. As I reached into the window to get my shoe, the outside punch, the security guard making his rounds on the prison grounds, appeared.

I managed to get my shoe and hid behind a tree bare ass naked.

The punch (Joe Witocziak) never saw me. He got back in his truck and left. I headed for my house with just my shoe in my hand.

If he would have seen me I know he wouldn't have believed one word of what I had to say about the situation.

The next day I got called down to see the boss, Deputy Superintendent Mindy.

"Haas, did you hear anything outside last night like broken glass?" Mindy asked.

"No," I replied and played it cool. "Why do you ask?"

"Because something broke my basement window."

I never sweated so much in my whole life, but until this book no one ever knew it was me.

CHAPTER 8

Underground Potato Peeling

The old prison was something else. I can remember being told that I was in charge of the potato peelers.

So one night Dirty Eddie, one of the older guards, told me what to do. He sent me off to get a small wooden box and a set of keys.

I returned to the kitchen and he gave me a list of peelers I had to pick up. So off I go to get these guys in Center Block.

When I got to Center Block and started lining up the 10 inmates, I started thinking about how many problems I could have with them by putting potatoes into a machine.

When I returned to the kitchen with this group, I was told what had to be done. I took the inmates into the basement below the kitchen, which had very bad lighting like an old Frankenstein movie.

They wanted 300 pounds of potatoes peeled. That was six, full 50-pound bags that had to be peeled.

We had to dump the bags into this machine and let them get peeled before transferring them into buckets of cold water when they were almost done.

Next, each potato has to have the eyes cut out and removed before taking them back to the kitchen. To do this, I had to give each inmate a small paring knife to remove the eye marks.

It meant I had to give each man a small knife out of the little box. Now ask yourself what is wrong with this picture, because I was doing just that at that moment.

Locked in with them in this hole, I wondered if I would ever leave the basement alive. I don't know why, but I never had a problem and I must have done this 50 times or more over the years.

I treated these men as people and treated them like you would want to be treated. Still, I may have had to remove shit stains from my britches every time after a trip to the basement.

CHAPTER 9

Taking Care Of The Boys

I had two favorite sergeants and they were the best of friends.

A little guy known as Sergeant Joe and the heavyset Sergeant Slimmer, also known as Cool Breeze.

If you saw one you would always see the other.

I never knew how Sergeant Slimmer got his name because he must have weighed over 300 pounds.

Sergeant Joe always said if you want respect from the inmates you have to give them respect. He also told me to always get back to an inmate if he had a problem. If an inmate asked you a question, it was best to get back to him even if the answer was no.

This let him know he meant something to you, so it was important to always answer him, and I did just that. This was the best advice I ever received and I believe that's why inmates respected me.

Sergeant Slimmer was a great guy. He took me under his wing and looked out for me as well as broke my balls all the time.

He had a great way with the inmates and always treated them with respect.

One time we had an old cook who had no teeth and we were feeding a jail block in the kitchen. Cook Gill was passing out the soup to about 90 inmates. He was in some kind of trance and almost half asleep, but he just kept ladling out the soup.

Then he drooled into the soup out of the corner of his mouth because he had no teeth.

The inmates saw this and began to scream, "HE SPIT IN THE SOUP!"

Sergeant Slimmer asked what was happening and I told him. He immediately ordered us to throw out the soup.

He said to give these guys all the peanut butter and jelly and cake that they want. Problem solved!

He said to always take care of the boys as it wasn't worth having a problem or creating a bigger one. Solve the problem in a simple way so the boys feel like they are somebody.

The sergeants took care of me and showed me how, whenever possible, that finding ways to take care of the inmates was the best solution.

CHAPTER 10

Prison Life Was A Burden On The Guards

Sergeant Schelmer was in charge of the kitchen and he mostly sat in the back room on a chair near an open window.

He only came into the kitchen to get the count and see if there were any problems.

I remember one winter day he sat there in the breakroom with the window open, sweating profusely, but sitting in three inches of snow inside the building. I never saw a man sweat that much. He was always wiping off his forehead with a hankie.

Sergeant Schelmer was a hell of a drinker.

Schelmer and Sgt. Joe would always stop at the VFW Post in Lancaster on their way home. One day about six or seven of us stopped at the VFW for a drink after work. We took up the whole corner of the bar.

A young man dressed in painters' clothes stopped in for a beer. He cut in between us and he had real long hair and put $5.00 on the bar.

Sgt. Schelmer looked over at Norm Ross, one of the guards.

"Hey Ross, you never introduced me to your wife," bellowed Schelmer.

Needless to say everyone laughed at the painter, who then left his beer and money on the bar and walked right out the door.

It was an innocent joke at the painter's expense, but we were unified. Everyone always looked out for one another. We worked in a sad and depressing environment, so we all needed to keep a good sense of humor and a smile on our faces.

I can remember the day Sgt Schelmer had his finger bitten off by an inmate. He was always so good with the inmates. He always put them first, so to have this happen to him was a shock.

He was never the same after that and went into a deep depression. One he could not return from. He mixed booze and pills and then I heard he jumped off a bridge onto the thruway and was killed by a car. This was a huge loss for our facility.

We lost many officers due to the excessive job stress that was just unreal. Many officers who worked for years were afraid of the job. They too often turned to booze or drugs to continue to work at the Erie County Correctional Facility.

CHAPTER 11

A Great Man
Gone Too Soon

There were guards who hated inmates and wanted to be big shots. I, however, enjoyed inmate contact.

I wanted to help them if I could but if they wanted to be an asshole, I'd be the first to treat them like one. I never felt like I had a problem that I couldn't solve. I was always willing to listen and hear them out. It costs nothing. Maybe I had big balls or maybe I was just lucky, but that was my approach.

One fellow correctional officer we lost was Dick Reed, who was also our next door neighbor.

We lived on the old prison grounds from about 1974-1985. These homes were great and priced very well, about $60.00 per month way back then if memory serves me correct. Dick was our neighbor. He had three boys, Keith, David and Tim. Doris was his wife and very pretty. They were a perfect family.

Dick was not a forceful person. He was an easy-going-kinda guy, which I admired, but he was the first officer I ever saw get hurt by the inmates. He was involved in a fight in the Young Men's Block and had a black eye, broken jaw, stitches, and had to have his jaw wired shut.

This incident happened on Christmas Eve. His boys had never really seen him hurt and didn't realize the dangers of the job. What a wake-up call for everyone.

The fear was now real for me. This is the kind of job where everything may go well for years and then all hell breaks loose. We worked on a wire every day.

So that's how Dick's day went that Christmas. This event changed him dramatically and stress really set in, and understandably so. He had served the county for years and then almost lost his life.

A few years later, Dick no longer lived on the prison grounds. One night he shoveled the snow off his car after a snowstorm so he could drive home. By the time he got home, he suffered a massive heart attack and died in his wife's arms in the doorway of their new home.

This was a great man, husband, father and friend. He's dearly missed. When I think about him I have to smile. We had great times together. His one son later became a correctional officer, following in his dad's footsteps.

CHAPTER 12

Tough As Nails
When Needed

Stress is something you can't put your finger on. It's different for each person. I can remember back about the summer of 1975. We used to have movies in the Chapel. This was a giant room with a stage that was used for church on Sunday and movies on Saturday. It was also used for meetings for officers or supervised family visits with inmates.

That summer, we had a young inmate who decided to have the inmates take over the Chapel. They held one sergeant and four officers hostage.

Our superintendent at that time was Mr. Frank Festa, and he had giant balls. When he found out he called in all the correctional officers. Everyone dressed in full gear, helmets and batons. He also called in the Sheriff Road Deputies in RIOT GEAR.

Mr. Festa had all the correctional officers line both sides of the hall, all the way back to four corners about 100 yards. He had the deputies hidden around the corner. When everyone was in place, he took two officers with him to confront the prisoners.

One of those guards was Walter Wateisek. He was a giant of a man, so much so his riot helmet was too small. It couldn't be pulled down to fit properly on his head.

They busted into the Chapel, and Mr. Festa told Robin, the instigating inmate, "You are not in charge any more. I am!"

He then instructed the rest of the inmates, about 200 of them, that they had 10 minutes to return to their cells. Once they saw the hallway lined with all of us, they jumped over each other to get back to their cells.

We did have to remove about six inmates, including Robin. Six of the inmates went to Segregation and Robin, who was a young man, went to the Young Men's Unit. He fought all the way. We had to drag him down the hall all the way to the Young Men's Unit. He was still fighting us as we were placing him into his cell.

I am sure he must have banged his head a few times along the way, but he would not stop trying to resist us. From that day on he was never the leader of the pack. He lost the starch in his pants after that episode.

Over the years I ran into Robin in and around the Buffalo area from time to time. He seemed to stay out of trouble after he was released. I know it was a scary day for the sergeant and the four guards that were being held.

The quick response that day from Mr. Festa was extraordinary. His only concern was for the sergeant and four officers being held captive.

He has always been one of my favorite bosses because if something like this happened again, you want to know that they are coming to get you. You definitely don't want them waiting like what happened in Attica.

CHAPTER 13

Hot Dogs And Hot Paint

Some of the stories that the old timers talked about from the 1950s were funny. I thought that they should not be forgotten, so I'll share two quick tales. Hopefully they will bring a smile to your face.

They used to tell a story about a Polish officer who was in charge of the kitchen.

When going home after a shift, the guards always walked through the front gate. The superintendent religiously watched the officers coming and going during the shift change.

On this particular day, the kitchen officer bumped his lunch box against the front gate and about eight pounds of hot dogs fell out. He looked at the Super and said, "I betcha someone is playing a trick on me."

You would be surprised at the stuff that was taken home by the COs that was pilfered over the years. We even had a CO that stole toilet paper. There was a saying that all the thieves are not on the inside.

There's another old story about the COs that were in charge of the paint gang. They had a fake paint can that could snap over another can. It had paint on the outside but it was a ruse.

They would take stew or soup from the kitchen and this worked for years. Until one day they picked up hot soup from the kitchen and crossed the yard on a cold winter afternoon with Buffalo's below-zero temperatures.

It was a nice clear winter day. About 15 minutes later Superintendent Redman called down and asked them what kind of paint was in the bucket.

"Paint?" replied the paint-supervising officer. "Why? Why do you ask?"

"Well," said Redman. "I was watching you guys cross the yard and it was the first time I ever saw steam coming from a paint can!"

CHAPTER 14

Rehabilitation Is Needed

The older COs were called HACKS and the younger correctional officers were called KEEPERS, just like at the zoo.

Prior to 1970, inmates could learn a job or a trade while on the inside. Some of the jobs were bakers, cooks, barbers, shoemakers, farmers, auto mechanics, painters, laundrymen, carpenters and bricklayers. Others could even work toward earning their high school diploma.

They wanted inmates to get out of prison with a trade or skill in hopes of turning their life around. The inmates had hope, but prisons have become more like giant warehouses.

Now we bring the guys in and try to keep them comfortable and occupied so that we don't have any problems.

When their time is up we just throw them back onto the streets no better off than when they came in here two years ago. What a waste!

The only help they have now is a high school diploma. For these reasons, too many prisoners came back like a revolving door.

Don't get me wrong, I know these guys are not angels, but to have a place to stay, food to eat and a family to care for, the things that make you whole, you need a job. And to get a job, you need to have a trade that pays you a decent wage.

If we can do this and make these guys feel worthwhile, they might make it. We need to help them, we need to stop the warehouse process. Maybe new and better programs would help like computer training and such.

CHAPTER 15

Not All Change Is Good

The older correctional officers have worked through different conditions over about a 30-year time span.

Prisoners had it hard and "doing time" was tough, but the new prison they built looks more like a high school. Inmates have no fear of going to jail or returning to this place.

Times used to be hard and we dealt with a firm hand when needed, but that has all changed to kid gloves.

The only deterrent for prisoners now is the food. It's so bad that most don't even eat it. They just throw it out. They live on Oodles of Noodles from the commissary or whatever else the commissary sells.

The quality of the food is poor, due to poor management. They do not check for quality or the quantity of food being served.

They do not change menus. It's just the same old shit week in and week out.

The kitchen also gets school lunch food, but most of the good stuff like turkey, pork, and fruit has disappeared over the last 15 years. One of the bosses ran his own catering service, so you know where that food went. Enough said.

The only deterrent to keep you out of prison is the younger inmates. They are wild, with no respect for parents, teachers, police, correctional officers or their fellow inmates.

So needless to say, you have to worry about your fellow inmates starting trouble with you, or stealing your stuff, like your sneakers, your radio or the food that you bought. This makes for a long bid.

It used to be that you could keep your room wide open and nothing would disappear. Your fellow inmates would help you and look out for you and everyone got along.

Now it is pressure all the time from the young men.

The old timers like to say I'm never coming back. What a different TIME. The old ones had respect for one another, but no more. There is just no honor among thieves these days.

CHAPTER 16

Free Riders Were Hard To Stomach

We had our share of Free Ride Officers, people who made a career out of being hurt. We had a sergeant who collected for more than seven years. He was a drunk in life and hurt numerous times.

One time he was at his cottage and wanted to get rid of the high grass and weeds. He poured gasoline all around on a hot day and went into his cottage to get a beer. When he came back out he lit a match to do the burn and he also lit his own ass on fire. What saved him was the nearby pond he jumped in.

He had real bad burns and had to keep black suave on his burns and was out about six months. I can remember being out and riding by his house and he was sitting on the porch. He looked like a mummy wrapped in gauze and black suave.

I stopped, told him I was going to the store and asked if he needed gas or anything.

"Fuck you, Haas" he yelled back.

Then there was the time he had an affair with the girlfriend of an inmate who worked for me in the commissary. This inmate, Ken, had a girlfriend and a son about three.

Ken was in jail for drag racing and hit another car and killed someone. His relationship seemed fine with the girlfriend and his son, until one day he showed me a picture of the two of them on vacation. His son was fishing in a pond and his girlfriend was standing next to him. In the background was Sergeant Red's cottage.

Sergeant Red met her on visits and they fell in love and were playing house. Not long after that the sergeant's affair was exposed and he lost his wife.

They then moved into his love nest on the prison grounds, and he had his cottage. He eventually got what was coming to him as she left him and took all the furniture. He came home to an empty house.

This was quite the joke around the prison for a long time. Can you believe a guy would put his coworker on the line? I had to work with Ken everyday knowing that the sergeant was fucking his old lady. Ken turned out to be an okay guy.

It didn't take too long after this that Sergeant Red drove down an embankment on Route 219, drunk again and almost died. He returned to work for a brief time only to blame his health on a fight at the facility, and then was off work for about six years. This is what I call a low life. He wasn't a good CO to begin with and was not missed one bit.

We had one officer that had been there more than 20 years but had not worked three years total. Now here is a guy who kept falling down on wet floors, at least three times that I can remember.

He can't wait to get back to work. He's never been late, because he doesn't work.

He makes other officers and employees look bad. He gets $47,000 from the county, $10,000 as a representative payee and a side job with the bank. He makes over $60,000 a year and only works part-time. I can't even bring myself to say hello to him.

Another officer was hurt on the job. She was driving inmates to a hospital in Buffalo and stopped the van to let ducks cross Genesee Street and was rear ended by a doctor. Damage was about $250 dollars, but according to her she will never be able to work a regular job.

51

So the county put her on light duty. After that, she couldn't work around inmates, was never ordered to work overtime, took her vacation when she wanted and spent her days cutting out coupons for $47,000 a year.

CHAPTER 17

We Always Remember The Good Ones

I could go on about the bad ones but you need to hear about the good ones, too! Some guys are a cut above the rest, the John Wayne types.

Exhibit A was Sergeant Bruce Parker who was involved in a fight with an inmate.

He wound up getting hit and took a couple of stitches to his head to stop the bleeding, but he was back at work the next day.

Then around Christmas we had a holiday party after work. On his way home, he went off the road and rolled his truck. He was hurt so bad they didn't think he would live, but Bruce was a strong willed person.

He hadn't been able to do much from the waist down since the accident, but he always talked about coming back to work in a wheelchair.

He earned the respect that he's given, not like some of the other wimps who looked for reasons to be off work. Bruce looked for reasons to get back to work, even in a wheelchair.

Life is a funny thing and unfair at times. Charlie Lang, a CO whom I had known for 20 years, passed away too soon. He was a person I would see four or five times a week.

He was only 56 years old, a big guy with big feet. His feet would arrive about a half hour ahead of him.

His favorite saying was WORD. We would all laugh when he said it and it's what he'll be remembered for most? Or does he just fade away? Does this happen to us all, people stand around and say what a great guy you were and then you're forgotten?

My dad always said, "As long as one person thinks about you that you're really never forgotten."

That's why I wanted to write this book, I wanted people to know that your life is very important. That you should enjoy yourself and try to help your fellow man as much as you can. You only pass through life once and you want to be remembered.

I want to be remembered as a man who was fair, loved his family, tried to help those that I could and always put a smile on people's faces.

CHAPTER 18

We Made Work Fun To Kill Time

I've had many fun times at work and if you can do this job with a smile it's better for everyone.

I had an inmate that worked for me all the time. His name was Steve Nemith. He came from New York City. He was about 54 years old and was a heroin addict, but a very good and trustful person. Every time he came back to jail he listed me as his next of kin.

The officer from the intake that processed him in would call me and say your son is here. He was about three years older than me! We've busted each other's balls for about 30 years.

He always showed up and worked hard for me. Although inmates are not supposed to talk about each other, he'd kind of let me know if a guy is an asshole or not, stealing from the commissary or if there is trouble in the prison.

I remember one time I had a young man working for me who was busted for selling drugs at the University of Buffalo (UB). He was shitting his pants about being in jail.

"Oh, you were busted for selling drugs at UB," said Steve. "Is that right kid?"

"Yeah," replied the newbie.

"Maybe you know my buddy."

"What's his name?"

"Peter Goesinya," replied Steve.

"I don't think so," replied the kid.

"Never mind. You'll know him tonight."

The kid was really scared then. When Steve left the room I told the kid he was just having fun with him.

Sometimes we'd take squirt bottles (for cleaning) and start a war. One time I soaked his crotch like he wet his pants and sent him up to the front office to see my wife.

He replied, "Boss, I can't go up there like this."

I told him it was a direct order. I called Marcia to warn her about Steve.

First thing she said to Steve, "I think you've been drinking too much coffee. It's starting to run through you."

We still laugh about that.

Another thing was Steve loved sweets. He'd come into the prison at about 168 lbs. and would go home about 210. We'd get him fat and sassy. He liked to steal chocolate cake from our bakery so one day we ambushed him with a sheet cake and made him wear it. He had cake in his hair, on his glasses, up his nose and so on. He wore it!

Mr. Gallagher, our superintendent, once told Steve he wanted a VCR and TV for a Christmas present. Now he must know that Steve makes his money on the street boosting (stealing from stores). Mr. G gave him a hundred dollars and told Steve to call him and he would pick it up.

Steve took the hundred, spent it on heroin and basically said, "Fuck You!"

Mr. Gallagher would call me every day and ask if I'd heard from my buddy Steve. The answer was always no.

Well, needless to say Steve got busted, so on his first day back going to medical, he stepped into my office. I heard the superintendent's voice in the hallway so I had Steve hide behind the door.

The Super stuck his face into my room.

"Your fucking buddy is here and I want my money back," said Mr. G. "He's a dead man walking."

He left and Steve steps out from behind the door and said, "I'm Fucked!"

"Yes you are," I confirmed. But all was forgiven by the Super once he chewed a piece of Steve's ass off.

I had many inmates who worked for me who were good: Ken, Mike, Rob, Smallwood, Fred, Joe, Steve, and one of the best was my Irish buddy Patty. They were all part of my gang. A lot of inmates wanted to be part of Spanky's Gang.

You got a little extra by working and you enjoyed yourself because time seemed to go by faster. People respected you for working your way through your bid.

CHAPTER 19

Spanky Is Born

You're all probably wondering how I got the nickname Spanky. Everyone thinks it's from the classic TV show, *Spanky and Our Gang*, but it came from an inmate in about 1974.

I was running the kitchen on Thanksgiving Day. All officers and inmates were fed and it was now time to clean up for the night.

It was about 6:30 p.m. and we were down to one inmate and myself doing pot and pans.

"Hey, let's get these pots done so I can go home and eat with my family," I announced.

"What if I don't," he replied. "What are you going to

do? You gonna spank me."

"YEAH!" was my reply and from that day on I have been known as Spanky.

This guy was released not long after and never came back, but that nickname stuck with me my whole life.

There were several officers with names much worse than mine.

There was Shaky, Blubber, Soft Talk, Bear, Red, Cool Breeze, Big John, Buck & Quarter, Cry Baby, Eat Em Up, Curly, Dead Bolt and Boogie. I could go on and on.

Mine has been around forever. I even had my license plates customized to read SPANKY.

You would be surprised how many guys I have seen while out shopping with my wife Marcia. I would never embarrass anyone I ran into that I knew from the prison. I would just let them talk and treat them like a friend.

I must admit that I love the name Spanky. I'm not sure why, I just think you're a little special when the guys give you a nickname and you have it for your entire life.

I always said if the guy who gave me this nickname ever came back that I was going to write up his ass. He never returned. He has no idea his handle has stuck for life.

CHAPTER 20

Nothing Was Ever A Piece Of Cake

I can remember my early days in the old place (the real prison). We had a gun room that overlooked the mess hall. We fed one block at a time for safety. The inmates walked into the mess hall single file through a double gate and it was locked behind them. A CO would stand in between the gates, and would instruct who could come and go into the kitchen.

The inmates would go through the line to get their food and go to their table and stand until they had three inmates so they could then sit down all at once.

You had two benches, one on each side of the table. All six would sit down together, so you would have six inmates at a table.

There was no talking and they could not trade food. They could get extra of everything except meat and dessert, but whatever extra they took they had to eat.

We had two officers in the mess hall and we had one sergeant that watched 50 inmates on each side, so we fed about 100 inmates at a time.

The gun room that overlooked the mess hall had one officer watching everything. He had a cabinet that held a gas rifle and four shells. Should anything happen in the mess hall upon the sergeant's command he would fire a round into the mess hall. That would settle things down and we would get more officers and remove inmates as needed.

The first time I was called in to work I was in bed. I was called in to work the 12:00 a.m. to 8:00 a.m. shift as they were short COs and needed help for breakfast.

Sergeant Grygo was in charge and he told me to take the gun room. You walked up a small set of stairs and sat looking onto the mess hall through a small bulletproof window.

It had small ports on each side so you could fire the tear gas rifle if needed. That day I couldn't stay awake. I was 23 and tired. My face fell against the window and my hat tipped up against the glass and I was sound asleep for about fifteen minutes. I had inmates looking at me, but they were not sure what my problem was.

After my shift manning the gun room, I soon realized the inmates weren't the only ones that noticed my face pressed up against the thick glass. I got called into Sergeant Grygo's office for a chat.

"Haas, the next time you decide to fall asleep," said Sergeant Grygo. "Could you do it leaning back in the chair so your face isn't pressed against the window?"

That was not my finest moment, but it was the last time I fell asleep on the job.

We also had the Tower job, where you had to inspect vehicles in and out of the prison. You had to have seniority to get this job.

One time I fell down some stairs at the prison and bruised my back and spleen. Since that happened while the regular officer on the day shift that manned the Tower was out sick for several days, they told me to take the Tower job from 8 a.m. to 4 p.m.

I thought it was going to be a piece of cake, but given my luck that was not the case. The first truck through that morning was a county garbage truck.

All you had to do was press a button and the gate went up and down. It had a large light just outside the gate that stayed red to stop and flashed green to go when the gate was clear.

Pretty simple operation to manage, but the driver of the garbage truck did not stop and drove right through the gate.

The gate was bent and damaged to the point that it was now out of order. The driver was an older guy. He just got out of the truck and shrugged his shoulders. If I had a bucket of shit I would have thrown it at him.

I had not notified my boss what had happened, but when he found out, I spent the rest of the day with a gun marching back and forth in front of the busted gate.

Turned out working the Tower wasn't the piece-of-cake assignment I had hoped it would be. The gate didn't get fixed until later that week, and what a week that was.

CHAPTER 21

Too Many Tragedies Without Notice

I can remember many deaths at the prison.

We had an inmate who choked on his own vomit. We couldn't clear his passage. He was playing basketball and must have over done it and wham, gone.

As I looked at him lying there I thought to myself he's someone's son or father and now he was gone. This occurred at the old prison. Sometimes life just doesn't seem fair.

We lost several inmates due to hanging at the new prison. We had a young man who received a phone call with news that his girlfriend and son were leaving the state. So at 20 years old he thought his world was over and hung himself.

I was the third man in the room when the alarm sounded. I knew he was dead even though they transported him to the hospital in an ambulance. About five minutes after the ambulance left the guy's brother showed up.

The young man obviously needed some psychiatric help and intervention but it was not detected by anyone. Once we put all the pieces together you could see why he was depressed. This was very sad that he thought his world was over and he wanted to die.

God never gives you more than you can handle even though it seemed heavy at the time. I wish he had talked to someone. Maybe someone could have talked him out of hanging himself. Maybe he'd still be with us today.

I also saw an officer lying dead in the yard, he died of a massive heart attack. Our medical staff tried to revive him but he was gone when he hit the ground.

It's such an odd circumstance to go to work one day and never make it home. This guy died at work.

As I get older, I know someday I'll be buying the farm. I want to leave something behind to help other people. I want to share my thoughts on how I see the world. I want people to remember me when I go, and maybe this book will help them remember me. Maybe it will provide some comfort.

CHAPTER 22

Fun While It Lasted

When I first came to work at the prison I had plenty of energy to burn, so I started pulling together an annual summer party.

During these gatherings we played a softball game for bragging rights. We had beer and hot dogs afterwards, and then teased one another until next year.

The officers with more than 10 years were on one team pitted against the officers with less than 10 years on the other team. The old timers were called the Bullfrogs and the younger crew were nicknamed the Tadpoles.

I'm standing (back row center) with my fellow guards after one of our softball contests.

Dick Hutton, a little short guy, was all spit and polish. You could see your face in his shoes. He was the captain of the Bullfrogs, but I remember their first loss to us after four years.

He cried and stood on a chair and announced that all Bullfrogs were not man enough. As part of the younger team, our guys ate that up. I never saw guys get along so well in my whole life.

We were bonding and seemed to all become one. We started working together and looking out for one another at work.

However, this would soon change as the old timers retired and the new younger COs moved in. Not all, but some had piss poor attitudes.

They knew all the answers. You couldn't tell them anything. Plus, they would report you if you did something wrong rather than let you know that you were doing something wrong.

Supervision loved it, but it was not a team effort. Not even close. The newer officers were only in it for themselves.

It used to be that the old timers ran a housing unit and everyone helped one another. But the new way is if you run a unit you have to run it your way and your helper just sits on his ass. They do not want to work. Most had never even had a real job before getting hired.

I guess this is a sign of the new generation. They want steady days with Saturdays and Sundays off. They want to pick their job and have first dibs on vacation days off.

There wasn't a single thing that they didn't know. They thought they knew everything. It didn't matter if you had worked at the prison for 40 years. It was unbelievable behavior on their part.

The thing that got to me is they actually referred to me as a dinosaur.

I even had a young guy call me Mr. Haas.

I turned around and said, "Mr. Haas is my dad."

It's odd how others see you sometimes. Those rather innocent words can make you feel as though your life has slipped away just a bit. Your steps get a little slower, your hair starts to turn gray, and all of a sudden 50-year-old girls start to look young to me.

You spend your whole life working and wishing you had time to retire. And when you're finally there, you realize that you wished your life away. This job definitely became less enjoyable toward the end.

Work can be a grind, but you gotta find a way to have fun in the margins. I loved busting balls with the inmates, of course in a good way, and that made the job fun. It made a tough job tolerable.

When you smile and have fun, you wish you had more time to go.

CHAPTER 23

Bittersweet Softball

I used to play a lot of softball on the outside. I played on three different teams about four days a week.

It got so bad my wife put her foot down.

"It's softball or me!" she demanded.

It took me a long time to make my final decision before we found a compromise.

"How about one team?" I asked.

"Okay," she said.

I was relieved.

Superintendent Frank Festa knew I played a lot of softball and asked me to bring in an outside team to play the boys.

Superintendent Frank Festa (standing on the mound) helped organize the game and served as the umpire.

I ran the idea by my team and they were excited to come into the prison and play against the inmates, so that was settled.

When the inmates heard the news you never saw such a happy bunch of guys.

They talked about it for weeks and even held tryouts. It was a pretty good team, too.

So on a hot day in June 1974, back during my early days on the job, we met on the caged in ball field. The superintendent was the umpire. When we started warming up on the field, we had a young kid about 20 on our team and he was shitting his pants.

Too many inmates to remember all of their names, but these two pictures show their smiles. Giving these men a few moments of normalcy was priceless and helped lower tensions between the guards and inmates.

He couldn't believe all the inmates in the yard, about 250 in total with only 15 officers standing guard and watching the game.

Our shortstop, one of my friends, Dan Moultrap said to the young guy, "Don't tie your shoes too tight."

"Why," responded the kid.

"Because you can't climb the center field fence with your spikes on if we win," Dan answered back.

We had a great day, played seven innings and beat the inmates, 6-4.

Afterward they picked on my team and laughed. We picked on them. It was like for two and a half hours, no one was in jail. It was just a group of men playing a softball game. We drank Kool-Aid and exchanged stories together.

The warden thanked us for coming and the inmates talked about the game for weeks.

 It seemed to take the bitterness out of the prison at least for a while.

For the next four years my team played our annual softball game.

CHAPTER 24

Fun And Consequences

In the summer of 1975 we wanted to have a party on the Fourth of July.

We had four different housing units and wanted to have an old-fashioned holiday party.

So a fellow CO and I talked to the warden about prizes and games. We had a rope pull with a borrowed rope from the local fire hall, three-legged races, ball games and the like. Prizes were cigars, cigarettes and candy.

Everyone enjoyed themselves. My co-party planner was a great guy and a great worker, and instrumental in getting the details pulled together. His only problem was the bottle. He would get drunk and then be on a hoot for about a week.

The funniest time was when he came back to work drunk as a skunk. The guys watched out for him, but when he entered the facility problems began.

I was running the kitchen and we had a room that the officers sat in for coffee and lunch. Well, I looked in and there he was. He couldn't even focus his eyes on me.

"I think I will go and get a haircut," he said, referring to the inmate-run barber shop.

"You know you can't get a haircut," I advised him. "You'll get your ass in trouble."

"Fuck them," he replied as he walked out and headed for the barber shop.

Fifteen minutes later, Lt. Grygo showed up in the kitchen looking for him.

"No sir," I answered when asked if I saw him and off he went.

It was about an hour later that I heard he was found and was sent home.

But as he left he backed into someone's car. Ouch.

Lt. Grygo sternly suggested that someone should drive him home.

He got five days off from work with no pay.

CHAPTER 25

Impaired Judgment

Dick had a motorhome we used to take to the Bills game. What a riot. We would get 10 to 15 guys and drink on our way to the game. Because we were all correctional officers we felt nobody would fuck with us.

When we got to the game and set up our tailgate area, we started cooking and drinking. Inside the stadium watching the game, we continued to drink. After the game, we retreated to the motorhome and drank some more.

Then on our way home, we still kept drinking.

Now a word to the wise, when you drink your personality changes

I can remember Dick was arguing and fighting with Ken, another officer. Dick told Ken, "to get in the motorhome," as we were getting ready to leave the stadium.

"Fuck you," barked Ken.

This went back and forth for 15 minutes as they exchanged pleasantries. Finally, Dick said goodbye and we drove off. Ken had to get his own ride home.

We kidded Dick for years because after that nobody would ride with him because they were afraid they'd have to walk home.

Two adults acting like kids. It's funny how drinking can make an asshole out of you, but looking back it was such great fun to watch.

About drinking and driving please take heed, do not drink and drive! It's not worth the problems it causes and you might end up in jail.

CHAPTER 26

A Hard Lesson Extracted

In my early days on the job back in 1972 we had a funny thing happen. An Indian who worked for me got drunk while on his work detail in the kitchen. He got himself locked up and had to go to our in-house court.

Mr. Meyers, the prison superintendent, was responsible for reading the charges to him.

He looked up and called for the Indian to enter the courtroom. When he entered he had a bandage over his right eye.

Meyers looked at him and said, "We have a report that you were drinking."

"Yes sir," confirmed the Indian.

"How did you hurt your head?" was the first question the superintendent asked.

"I was so drunk that I fell out of bed and hit my head on the toilet bowl," admitted the Indian. "I will never drink that orange extract again."

Upon hearing his explanation, Meyers asked the inmate to step outside.

Then Meyers looked around the room and smiled. He never smiled.

"Is that like the vanilla extract we drank in the Navy?" he asked. "I think this guy learned his lesson. Bring him back in."

The inmate returned and nervously awaited his fate.

"Go back to your cell and don't do this again," instructed Meyers. "I do not want to see you back in court. Time served!"

"Thank you," said the Indian.

You better believe he didn't show up again.

CHAPTER 27

The Sweet Smell
Of A Jailhouse Bust

When I got a booze bust in jail, it would give me goosebumps. I loved to find that stuff.

When you make booze all you need is bread, sugar, yeast and Kool-Aid or fruit. As it ferments you must bleed the plastic bag or pail. That is to let the air out, but that air smells great like a trip to a winery.

Many times I found their stash because they just bleed the bag.

I remember one time I was taking head count in the Young Men's Block and as I was walking down the gallery I could smell wine. I walked back and forth between three cells to pinpoint the culprit.

"What's up," said the inmate as I stared into his cell.

"Pick up your boxes," I instructed him.

He had two boxes and picked them both up by holding the bottom.

Inmates often kept boxes in their cell and used them like furniture. It kept their personal items off the floor and they usually laid towels over them.

"Now pick up those boxes again but don't hold the bottom," I commanded.

As soon as he picked them up, a big plastic bag filled with homemade wine fell out.

I took the bag to the officer in charge for evidence for court. I put it under Lt. Grygo's desk, filled out the paperwork for court and left.

About two hours later I got a call from the lieutenant who wanted to know what was in the bag under his desk.

"Yes sir," I said. I was all big and happy getting ready for them to give me an Atta-Boy Medal.

But he cut me off before I could explain, "I want you to see this."

I went to his office and the bag had fermented and half of his desk was off the ground.

"Another hour and we would have had wine all over the room," he said.

The bag was one of those milk bags with the hose on it, so I tied a knot in the hose to keep it from leaking out.

I did the opposite of what I should have done, which trapped the fermentation gas and could have caused the container to explode. Luckily that didn't happen, but that event taught me to never seal the bags or buckets until after they had fermented out the gas.

Those were great days on the job learning to be a correctional officer.

CHAPTER 28

Pranksters On The Run

Back in the day we had our own bakery and a baker who looked more like Sid Caesar than Sid did. He had a small notepad that he used every day to mark down how many days he had left to retire.

He was wishing his life away, but what a good sense of humor this guy had. Leonard Kozlowski was his name, but he was also known as Duke the Baker.

One day we were getting ready to leave, about six officers were sitting in the bakery waiting to go, so we couldn't let an opportunity go to waste.

When Duke the Baker was changing from his bakery clothes to his civilian clothes, as he started to put on his pants, I took a straw broom with the long end and hooked his pants. I then ran around the bakery holding his pants up in the air like a flag.

He was running behind me with just his socks and underpants. He chased me all the way down the hallway almost to the front gate.

I don't think I ever laughed as hard in my whole life as I did that day.

The officer at the gate shouted, "What the fuck is going on?"

Another time when we were sitting in the bakery waiting to go home, there was a small group of officers, a teacher and Duke.

The teacher started talking some shit about what he was going to do.

Then me and another officer grabbed this asshole and threw him up on the bread table, which was a big table used to cut and weigh the dough before baking the bread.

We pulled the teacher's shirt up and his pants down and took two loaves of bread and rubbed them on his chest and the crack of his ass.

When he got off the table he had crumbs all over himself. Then, surprisingly, he started talking shit again.

"He doesn't want white bread," I joked to the other officer. "He wants wheat bread!"

So it started the ritual all over again. He screamed and we were all laughing.

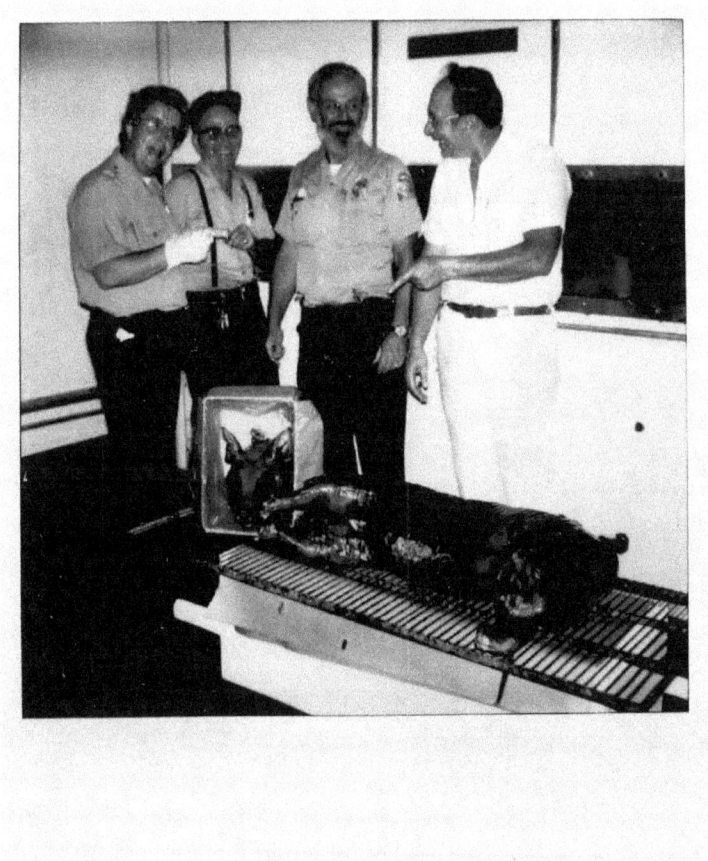

Sharing a few laughs during a pig roast at the prison. Pictured from left to right, me with fellow correctional officers Norm and Dick, standing alongside Duke the Baker.

CHAPTER 29

Character Is More Than Skin Deep

Back in the early 1980s, Joe Migliore was a young CO working with us. He was one handsome dude. My wife couldn't believe how good looking he was, but he was a down to earth great young man.

When my dad passed away he stopped at our house and dropped off about 10 bottles of booze. It was a great gesture, and the kid did it because he said he knew we'd be having people back to our house. Joe had such a big heart.

In life, you don't really know who your friends are

until something knocks you down. Those that show up in your worst moments are the most valuable ones. My dad was 62 when he passed, and it hit me hard. It probably hits most people hard, and it's a tough ordeal. Joe's support was never forgotten.

I remember one time Joe was talking some shit to us, so we were forced to retaliate. We could not let that stand. So we would take off his shoes and then throw them out the door to the outside recreation yard.

He would be standing there in the Young Men's Block with his uniform on and no shoes.

"You're out of uniform, Joe!" Sergeant Knappa would always say when he saw him.

It was so funny. And it's a good thing that the sergeant had a sense of humor and went along with it.

Little did we know, Joe had a drive inside of him and he wanted to be a New York State Trooper. He spent about four years with us and took the Trooper test and passed with a high score. And that didn't surprise us one bit.

He left us and became a Trooper. I saw him about 18 years later and he didn't have a hair on his head. He was the Michael Jordan of T Troop.

CHAPTER 30

Eternal Lessons From Dad

My folks split up when I was 12 years old. My mom took me and my two brothers with her to her new apartment, along with her new boyfriend.

Every chance I got, I would go back to my dad's place, until my mom finally just let me stay with him. My dad and I were the best of friends.

When I was 18 years old I started dating Marcia, who was two years younger. She was beautiful and we were madly in love with one another. My dad loved Marcia, too, and soon after we were going to have a baby. I was 19 and Marcia was 17.

My dad said he would babysit any time and we

could go out and be teenagers.

Then when my dad found out that I got the job as a correctional officer, he was the proudest guy in the world. I loved my dad. He was the best dad ever!

I can remember the day he passed away. I was at work at about 9:00 a.m. and I got a phone call from Marcia. She said there was a problem and asked me to come home.

My first thought was maybe something happened to one of my girls. She assured me the girls were alright, but she needed me to just come home.

I got permission to go and ran all the way home. When I got to the back door she told me my dad had passed away. This was a huge shock. I just couldn't believe it.

I knew he wasn't feeling the greatest. He and my mom had gotten back together, and they just returned home from visiting my baby brother Mick.

Mickey was doing time at the State Penitentiary for burglarizing homes. My dad was getting ready for work and had a heart attack. He fell into the bathtub and died.

I had the job to tell my girls that Grampy had passed away. I then had to call and tell Mick the news, and it really hit home with him because they had just visited him. He felt responsible and thought he might have had something to do with his passing.

The State gave him a five-day pass and released him under my custody. He had to get on a plane and I had to pick him up at the airport. Unfortunately, Mick had a drinking problem and couldn't get himself sober for very long.

My other brother, Robin, who I am the most proud of, also managed to get home. Robin was a well-known chef in Miami, Florida.

Robin had been through hell, too. My mom really screwed my brothers up when she took them to live with her boyfriend. Robin had to see a psychologist to get himself together. We became very close and I love him very much. He got married to a great gal who loves and understands him.

I was surprised how many people came to my dad's funeral. We had probably 80-100 people attend. This changed my outlook on funerals.

It underscored just how important it is for people to meet one another and exchange pleasantries and stories about their loved ones.

It means so much to the grieving family that others will miss their family members, too.

Please take time and attend funerals. I now understand just how important this is for the grieving family. That's enough about my dad. We always put flowers on everyone's grave, from my dad, my mom and my grandparents to my cousins and so on.

CHAPTER 31

The Old Prison
Was Self-Sufficient

The old prison was built in 1923 and back then it was built by the inmates. That approach continued over the years as lots of tasks were accomplished by using the inmates.

Every summer sometime in July we would open the cannery and what a job that was! The prison had an adjacent working farm used to grow green beans, potatoes, tomatoes, cabbage and corn. We would feed the cattle that we used for meat and milk at the facility, and we also raised pigs for food.

When the cannery opened in July, we'd start canning most of our vegetables. We had homemade crates that were stamped E.C.C.F., which stood for Erie County Correctional Facility. The picking crews used these crates to harvest and then the cannery crews would can the vegetables.

When you drove down the road all you would see were inmates working. I still have one of the old branding irons we used to stamp the wooden crates.

The cannery was in the basement under one of the housing units. It was just like out of an old movie, with pulleys, water, steam, rollers and metal cans.

If you were sent there you'd be peeling your balls off for about two to three weeks. Each inmate was given a knife and two inmates would sit on benches facing each other with a can in between them. They had to fill that can and then get another.

When I was sent down there it was to relieve another officer so that he could go home, and when I reported to the cannery officer Norm Walters gave me some valuable advice.

"Kid, when the steam comes up, stand behind these water tanks," said Walters.

Sure enough the steam came up and Norm pulled me back by him. I could hear squishing sounds, but when the steam went down the inmates were all still peeling.

Looking again I could see spots on them, dripping from their head, arms, and shirts. They would war with one another when the room steamed up and blocked our view. You couldn't see anything, but you could hear the tomatoes being thrown.

I stepped outside for air when Lt. Kopinski was on his way down the steps to go into the cannery. He was always in a hurry, so I said hello as he opened the door. Just then the steam came up inside and out the door came a tomato and hit me square in the chest.

Lt. Kopinski looked at me and smiled.

"That's why I held you up," I told him.

Yep, one big red spot and seeds on my shirt for the rest of the day. I went back in and everyone was peeling tomatoes. This canning was something to see.

We were self-sufficient. We made a lot of our own food. After the items were canned, we stored them in tunnels under the prison. During the winter we would go down and get them as needed.

CHAPTER 32

Many Things Soured Over Time

Times have certainly changed. After years on the job, we'd get paid big money for working overtime and we had guys fighting to get overtime. Depending on the day you could make $35 to $75 an hour.

In the old days you'd get a piece of paper that stated you worked an hour over. In return you'd get an hour off when they wanted to give it to you. Oh, you'd also get a free steak dinner if you were ordered to work an extra eight hours, but you could read the newspaper through that steak. I've seen cold cuts that were thicker.

The thin steaks aside, the food in the old place was great. You could get all you wanted to eat, but you had to eat what you took. For the holidays we had real turkeys, stuffing and gravy, mashed potatoes and homemade pies and ice cream.

All the meals were very good; hot soup, mashed potatoes, corn, applesauce, stew, homemade bread and rolls, hamburgers, sweet rolls, pies and doughnuts. It was all good food and they basically kept the same menu for 15 years.

It seems that things went downhill. People just stopped caring about doing a good job. No one took pride in the job or work they were doing. It's all about the money.

Now we have baloney about three days a week and the boys eat pre-made tacos, pizza, turkey-rolled meat and instant potatoes. It's all like fast food now.

They don't even check the food that's sent here and nothing is refused. It even seems like the bosses don't care either. Nothing gets weighed, so they don't know if they received 80 pounds of hamburger or 100 pounds. The prison could lose a lot of money in a year with this sloppy approach.

One day there was a knock on my door, so I opened it to see the delivery man standing there. He informed me that he had forgotten 20 pounds of stew that was part of the order, but the prison signed off and away he went. He was an honest man, but this underscored the poor management and lack of accountability in receiving shipments.

Please, if you have a good job, give it your best. Be proud of what you do and put your heart and soul into it. That's a dying breed, but a goal everyone should strive towards.

I always wanted to do a great job wherever I worked at the prison. Marcia and Marlo are the same way, cut from the same cloth, always striving to do their best. I always wanted the prison to succeed no matter who was running it.

There are some people that feel like the world owes them a living and they want everything for nothing. Leave everything for the next guy to do, get by with doing the minimum amount of effort.

Why not just help your fellow worker, jump in the mix and give a helping hand. That's the way it was 30 years ago when I started and the workplace was a much happier place.

The classic cover-your-ass philosophy seemed to ring truer with each passing year, but in the old days everyone worked together and had each other's back. The guys you worked with looked out for one another. It was a fraternity of brotherhood.

CHAPTER 33

Never Let Your Guard Down

I can remember working in the Segregation Unit in the old place. I was a new officer and this was a three-floor unit. They put all the problem inmates on all three floors.

These were the problem children in our facility. We had two rooms on each floor that we called the red, blue and white rooms. They had no bathrooms, just buckets. No water! What horrendous body odor and stench throughout the area.

We put one troublesome inmate in the blue room. Our medical staff warned us that he was certified and to be extra careful. So needless to say we watched him very closely. We had small port holes so you could keep an eye on him.

He was small and only wearing his underpants. He tore off the clothing part and was only wearing the elastic band.

He would break a plastic cup in half and would threaten us with it. Stand there with his balls and peter hanging out, and he was only four-foot tall.

Now the blue room had two doors leading to it, and two peep hopes that you watched through the walls. I was working with Officer Al that day.

"Kid," said Al as he turned to me. "We're gonna have some fun with this guy today."

We took turns opening the two doors to the blue room to keep him on notice.

Every time a door opened, this inmate said, "I know you two motherfuckers are coming for me. Well, I got something for your big white asses."

He would then hold out the plastic cup like he was holding a knife.

"I could cut you with it," he yelled.

We kept this up for a while off and on, but the shift changed and then we were off duty.

I was gone for a few days, but I was assigned to the Segregation Unit once again a few days later. I returned and started taking the head count and making punches on all three floors.

Then I went and checked on the blue room. I stepped inside when I didn't see anyone, but then I caught something out of the corner of my right eye. I kind of jumped a little as it startled me. It was our troublesome inmate up on the bars like a monkey but not moving. I poked him with my finger and he didn't move. He was very dark and his legs were hanging through the bars and you could see a thin white line in his eyes. He was barely breathing.

I called medical and when they checked the records they found he was supposed to get a shot to calm him down. One shot for the week but he had gotten one both shifts. He was close to death but luckily he survived. He was still wearing the elastic band and had the plastic cup in his hand.

It wasn't too long after this incident that I had a very serious problem with this same inmate. I was working in the Segregation Unit again, this time with Officer Ken, a pretty good-sized guy with a calming voice.

"Whatever you do, do not let him out of the blue room unless we are together," Ken warned me as he went on break.

Well needless to say as soon as he left this inmate wanted to use the toilet. It had been approved for him to use the bathroom in the presence of both officers. We were authorized to let him out of the blue room so he could shit in the real toilet in the gallery.

When I let him out he became wacked again. He would not go into the gallery and just wanted to walk around, even on our cat walk. I had to wrestle him to the floor just as Ken showed up and helped me place him back in the blue room.

He then looked at me sternly.

"Let this be a lesson that you carry with you for the rest of your career," said Ken. "Do what you are told, make sure you have help and do not take chances."

I did and he never said a word to anyone about this incident.

CHAPTER 34

A Solution For Every Problem

Another inmate we had in the Segregation Unit was a heavyset and lazy kid we'll call Chunky. He was an officer's nephew, and he was a major pain in the ass, but boy could this kid eat.

He always wanted a lot of attention. One day when I was making my punch on the second floor near his room I noticed he was just lying there on the floor. Normally you'd call for help and have him checked, but I just kept making my half-hour punches. After about five rounds he was sitting up on his bed.

"You don't give a fuck about me," he yelled when I was within earshot.

"I do, but not when you play these kid games," I told him.

I can remember around 1973 we got a new inmate on the second floor. He sounded like a white guy even though he was black. He fooled Chunky and convinced him that he was a motorcycle dude, belonged to a gang and was white. He could do this because he was on the opposite side of the gallery.

Well, Chunky sent him all kinds of food for about two weeks and called him his buddy. Then one day he asked me if that guy was white or black. I told him that his new friend was black.

"You motherfucker," he shouted at me.

"You're an asshole," I yelled back.

The worst time in the Segregation Unit was when the psychologist met with a group of about 10 inmates on the second floor all together.

They blamed their moms and dads for their problems. They would all be talking at the same time and then the yelling began. All of a sudden chairs started flying and the doctor went under his desk. It was bedlam.

I ran to the stairs and yelled for help!

We carried no radios, no clubs, nothing. Your only choice was to reach a phone and call for help, and it was like this for years. I had Lt. Lords at the door with a dozen officers within minutes.

I told him what had happened and by this point inmates were running around on all three floors.

"Catch them, throw them in the nearest cell and we will sort this out later," commanded Lords.

We had everyone locked up, but the last guy was on the third floor. So we surrounded him and as we all got near him, he looked at us and said, "You're all Viet Cong."

The doctor who was under the table suddenly joined us and tried to step in.

"He thinks you're all VC. I will handle this," said the doctor.

"You will like hell," Lords shouted back. "You fucked things up enough. We will handle it now so get out of our way."

Lt. Lords always carried a towel with him and I found out why on that day.

He would twirl the towel until it became almost like a rope, then he would wrap it around the inmate's throat and twist it until it cut off the air supply and he fainted. It worked great. It was a very effective way of subduing an out-of-control inmate, but I never used this approach. I was too afraid of injuring someone if I accidentally used too much force.

Now we're moving toward the last inmate with Lt. Lords in the lead. The inmate who was black and muscle bound looked right at Lords.

"VC!" he shouted. "You're all VC!"

Lords barked right back, "VC my ass. Get in that cell."

"Okay," he replied and quickly stepped inside without incident.

We then proceeded to put inmates back in the cells where they belonged. Lt. Lords was the best. He knew what was what. He had a solution for every problem.

CHAPTER 35

Learning To Take Charge

I can remember another time when I was running the kitchen.

I had an inmate that I needed to sweep and mop the kitchen.

"That's not my job," the inmate said, bucking my orders.

When you're new on the job, probably any job, but definitely when you're working in a prison, you don't always have a good answer for the backtalk.

So I took the inmate into the officer's mess hall where Lt. Lords was having lunch.

"Could I bother you for a moment?" I asked.

"What's the problem, Haas!" he responded.

I told him what happened and that the inmate was a cook, but I needed something done and he refused, telling me that it wasn't his job.

Lt. Lords looked at the inmate, or maybe I should say he looked right through the inmate. His stare was intense.

"Whatever this officer tells you to do is your job," Lords said as he never minced words. "You do whatever he says."

I went back to work and never had a problem again. And I used that statement in all areas of my job over the next 30 years.

CHAPTER 36

Scared Of Our Own Shadows

I remember one time I had to work with a sergeant that we called Super Cop, Lurch and Frankenstein. His problem was he wanted to be important even though he wasn't.

He thought he was a super sleuth, so we went out into the fields wearing camouflage clothes to spy on the inmates that were working in the fields.

The sergeant thought the inmates were up to no good. He thought they were having sex and getting booze or drugs. He thought we'd catch them in the act.

So Super Cop put me in the fields lying down among the tall grass and trees with a pair of binoculars. I had a great view of the inmates, but being the city kid that I am, I got bored being out there and staring for hours on end.

I spotted this large hole in the ground and began to watch it. It had some fresh dirt inside so I knew something was living there, but wasn't sure if rabbits, foxes or snakes called this place home.

Then suddenly out of the hole came this big, round furry thing.

We both spotted one another at the same time and briefly froze before running in different directions.

I crossed the field and headed to the prison (in record time) and told them this was my last time working in the fields. It was too much for this city boy.

Oh, and by the way, it was a huge woodchuck that emerged from that hole. And it definitely cast a shadow. The size of it gets bigger each time I tell the story.

CHAPTER 37

Never A Free Ride

In the old prison we used to take inmates in from Immigration. We would make sure that they were showered and dressed, then we'd place them in a special wing to wait for their hearing.

A lot of them would be deported, but if they had money the U.S. would always make them pay for their way home.

One time when I was on Immigration Duty we had to pick up and transport three Chinese guys to their hearing. Afterwards we returned them back to the receiving room so they could change back into their street clothes.

As they were getting changed, I noticed a guy fidgeting with a metal sign that read:

Remove your shoes.

Tie shoes together.

Keep your eyes closed.

I know this sounds a little weird, but they had to keep their eyes closed because we sprayed the inmates back then to kill bugs. You never knew what they might have brought into the country with them.

Turned out these guys had hid a thousand dollars behind the sign. We confiscated it and turned the money over to Immigration to help pay for their trip back to China.

If illegal immigrants had money, then they would have to use it to pay for their own deportation and trip home. That's why they hid the money.

CHAPTER 38

Be Fair And Honest

We had two officers in charge of the mess hall, Clean Eddie and Dirty Eddie.

Dirty Eddie had moves that tricked inmates into working, that's how he got his name.

Clean Eddie was a foul mouth who was always swearing at inmates and calling them motherfuckers. He was always pushing and shoving them. He ruled by intimidation.

But I remember the day that changed.

I was working in the kitchen and I was instructing each inmate how to return his silverware into a wash bowl and empty the leftovers into a garbage can. Clean

Eddie stepped up to an inmate and punched him on the arm. The inmate put his silverware into the bowl, emptied his garbage, put his tray down and then turned and punched Eddie hard in the chest.

Eddie looked up at me and said, "I am writing him up and you're my witness."

"I'm going to write you up Eddie because you hit him first," was my reply.

Lines were drawn and we never had anything to do with one another after that incident. Clean Eddie was a low life and did not know how to deal with people.

His son, we'll call him Little Eddie, came to work at the prison about a year after me, but he was a clone of his dad. He became a sergeant, but he was not very good when it came to dealing with people either.

One time he overheard me say an officer wanted to borrow my hat for uniform inspection. I wouldn't do it because I believed you should have your own things. But later that day Sergeant Little Eddie came into my office and wanted to know who was asking to borrow my hat. I said you'll have to find out on your own.

I remember a party we had at a local bar after work. Little Eddie smacked his wife right in front of everyone and four guys took him outside and kicked his ass. Women are crazy for staying with guys that abuse them. Life should be sweet and women have rights too.

Then there was Sergeant Benny, who looked a little like a fat Roy Rogers, but was a dirty prick, too.

We had a prison-wise inmate Willie, who was a booster on the streets. He stole clothes, shoes and whatever he could from stores. Sergeant Benny hated Willie with a passion. He tried to set Willie up by giving money to an inmate who in turn gave the money to Willie, so upon leaving the mess hall he pulled Willie out of line to jam him up.

Willie had been working in the kitchen serving food and was returning to his unit. Sergeant Benny told me to shake him down, but we found nothing.

"Where's the money, Willie?" Sergeant Benny asked.

"I threw it in the dumpster behind the kitchen," replied Willie with a big smile.

"Then you can crawl in and find it," snapped Sergeant Benny.

"If you want it bad enough you can climb in and find it yourself," Willie countered.

At this point Sergeant Benny dragged me into it.

"Haas, I'm going to write him up and you're my witness," he instructed.

"I will have to say you tried to set him up then sir," I answered back.

The issue was dropped. Nothing ever happened from this incident.

I really never understood what the hell this was

supposed to prove. I am a firm believer that the right approach was to be honest and do right by everyone, no matter whether they were a guard or an inmate.

I always tried to be fair and honest and figured the inmates would respect me for how I handled things. It would also make it easier for the inmates to accept punishment without a problem if they thought they were treated fairly.

Willie became a believer that I was an honest correctional officer.

CHAPTER 39

Look For The Best In Everyone

I ran into Willie twice outside the prison.

The first time, Marcia and I were out shopping. I was looking into a window of a leather coat store and there was Willie on his knees trying to undo the locks on the coat rack.

I snuck up behind him and his partner. When she saw me standing there her eyes got real big. Just then Willie jumped up not knowing who was there. He looked relieved to see it was me.

"Hey, Spanky," he greeted me with a big smile. "My

man Spanky!"

"Willie, I got someone I want you to meet," I said, so we stepped outside.

"So this is your lady?" asked Willie with a smile as I introduced him to Marcia. "Nice to meet you. Spank, what size is she?"

We both laughed.

"Willie, you're getting too old to be doing this stuff," I said.

"I know," he confessed.

The other time we met was at Penney's. I was paying a bill and he snuck up behind me. He put his hand against my back and yelled, "This is a stick up!"

Everyone bolted from the counter, as his booming voice sent anyone within earshot scattering for cover. We both laughed and hugged.

Willie had a great smile and a voice like Louis Armstrong. We had a great understanding and connection from his time in prison. He's passed on now, but I only need to shut my eyes to see him.

CHAPTER 40

Some Picks Were Better Than Others

Mike was another inmate with a drug problem. He would steal to support his drug habit. He would get caught and come to jail and I would bring him to work for me.

Boosters were the best workers. I would make sure they got enough to eat and they would make sure no one was getting anything over on me and the commissary.

Mike was depressed the first time I met him, his wife and child were out there and he was the provider now in jail. His wife's dad wanted to make Mike an honest man. He wanted Mike to do home repairs, but Mike wanted nothing to do with that. I tried to get Mike to do what was right and we had long talks and bonded over time.

I liked him because he had this great sense of humor hidden inside of him that I could easily bring out. We would laugh together and this helped his time pass while in prison.

He played a joke on a fellow inmate, Steve Nemith. Steve always played the football pool out of the paper. He would try and get the most winners for the week. He was hoping to collect the cash prize out of the Buffalo Evening News.

Needless to say he never won and we would all listen to how close he came every week.

Mike decided he would make up a letter to look like it came from the Buffalo Evening News. I slipped it into the regular mail in the unit for that night.

Mike's cell was next to Steve's, so he had a front-row seat when mail was passed out at lock down. The officers would just slide mail under the door.

"Fuck them and fuck that," Steve yelled upon reading the letter. Mike could hear Steve bitching and carrying on.

When they were later allowed to come out of their cells, Steve showed Mike the letter he received from the Buffalo Evening News. The letter said:

Please do not send any more picks because your picks were terrible. You stand little chance of winning. You are wasting your time and ours.

"Who the fuck are they?" asked Steve to Mike. He was still fuming, but Mike couldn't keep a straight face and started laughing.

"I suppose you and Spanky are behind this you fucks!" said Steve, realizing he'd been had and we were picking on him. We laughed about this one for years.

CHAPTER 41

The Family Business

Another good guy was South Buffalo Mike. He was a drinker and a fighter, and had a face that looked like he never won a fight on account of the fact his nose had been broken many times.

One time he was beaten up by guys with pipes. He was in the hospital ready to enter God's Kingdom, but he pulled through as it wasn't his time.

You could not have a better person working for you. He looked out for me as an officer and let me know what was up. Most of the officers didn't like him just for the way he looked or because he was outspoken but honest. I liked him for his honesty.

We became like cement over the years, sticking together and strong. When I heard about his wife, Susie, passing away, Marcia and I attended the funeral.

It's a sad thing to know a couple that had an up-and-down relationship as they've wasted a lot of time fighting when they could have been loving one another. They really loved one another, too. I pulled for Mike to recover and put his life back together.

The best (or should I say worst) family we ever had in prison consisted of four brothers and two cousins - Albert, Merle, Mike, David, and their cousins, Jimmy and John. The cousins were in and out and were just kind of burnt out, drop outs.

Albert was something else, he escaped three times. Known in the paper as Adventurous Albert of Alden. Once he stowed away under a garbage truck, but was found a short time later.

The second time he climbed a wall in the recreation yard. When Sergeant Clark saw what he was up to, he ordered him to come down.

Albert responded to that by yelling, "Fuck you, Clark!" just before he jumped the wall. Again, he was caught a short time later.

The third time was when he was on a work detail, but he wasn't on the loose for very long.

"Hey Al, you worry me," I said after he was returned back to the prison.

"Don't worry," replied Albert. "I wouldn't do that to you, Spank."

Thank God! That was a relief for me.

He owned a junkyard and dealt with car parts, tires and used autos.

Merle looked like a skeleton and had no respect for anyone. He was a master planner and was always thinking how he could get it over on people. I had him work for me twice, but some people just cannot handle trust. He shoplifted in the commissary, so I always kept a close eye on him.

Mike was a good kid who just needed to get spanked when he was younger. I liked this kid. Anything I asked him to do, he would do it. He had a booming loud voice. We got along really well and I never had a problem with him.

We had these family members at different times over the years when they weren't doing State bids.

CHAPTER 42

Actions Speak Louder
Than Words

We had this one lieutenant who was appointed to his rank. The inmates referred to him as Fred Flintstone, as some said his arms were sewn-in backwards because of the way he walked. He had a hair lip hidden by his beard and the lowest self-esteem of anyone I ever met.

He liked to sell himself as being important and was a know-it-all type. Truth of the matter is that he was a user. If he needed something he was all over you and when he didn't you were done.

He had no college or no special trades, but he was a smooth talker. He even had the superintendent fooled to leave him in charge when he was gone.

Lt. Flintstone had very little contact with the inmates because he couldn't deal with them. In fact, he didn't deal well with our civilian staff or many of the officers. It was either his way or no way of doing things. In reality, I believe he was a lonely man.

In all the years working at the facility I never pretended to be someone I was not. I was happy being an officer with Saturdays and Sundays off to spend time with my family. I did the best I could with my marriage and loved Marcia and the girls. I raised my children to be honest and respectful of others.

When I became an officer, I always treated the inmates with respect, but if they didn't want to return it, then I could play their game, too.

When I wrote an inmate up I didn't add charges to the list, I only wrote up what he did, I never added any charges or piled on the inmate. When he went to court, whatever he got was on him. I never asked another officer to verify something he didn't see. Nor would I sign a false statement for them. However, that was done by many officers.

"Whose side are you on?" I was once asked by a new officer that transferred in from Attica.

"The right side," I responded.

Think for yourself, don't be intimidated, be honest and tell the truth. I always told my gang (inmates) that they were responsible for their own actions. They were responsible for what they did. If they would have just thought for a minute before they acted, they could have changed their life. Maybe they wouldn't have ended up in jail.

CHAPTER 43

Comical Escapes

We had an escape at the old prison, and at the time we didn't have a great plan in place.

We knew everyone had to be locked down, but the officers spent about 45 minutes bumping into each other, like a *Three Stooges'* movie.

The sheriff showed up with bloodhounds, which seemed like a good idea. The dogs sniffed the inmates bedding and were off, out the front door and down the road. The sheriff, who weighed about 300 pounds, couldn't keep up. He fell down, lost his gun and hat and let go of the dogs.

Once he finally picked up everything and collected

himself, we headed out in pursuit of the escapee. We could hear the dogs baying like a werewolf at the moon ahead of us.

There were approximately 15 officers who lived on the prison grounds, and that was the direction we were headed.

As he was sensing victory, the sheriff confidently yelled out, "We got him cornered!"

But when we got to the house we found out it was a false alarm. The home had a young basset hound that was in heat. I guess if I were a bloodhound I would have done the same thing. Well, the escapee was eventually caught at his home a few days later.

Another funny escape was at the new prison, which was supposed to be escape-proof.

We did keep illegal immigrants that were caught at the prison, and I guess they didn't like that too much. These six Chinese men escaped by pulling their window out. It appeared that the bars ran through it, but they were only in the double pane window.

Only eight screws held the window in place, so they pulled it out and were off to the races. They stole a car, but didn't make it too far. The State Police picked them up on the New York State Thruway after they ran out of gas.

The strangest escapee story was a head-scratcher. This inmate escaped with only two days left on his sentence. He hopped the wall and was gone, but was caught in Buffalo two days later. Why did he do that?

Escapes happened in a variety of "clever" ways.

We once had an inmate escape who was working on the farm. He was running down the railroad tracks towards Buffalo and was picked up by Lancaster Police. He told them he was just out for a morning jog before he started milking the cows. He actually managed to make it about six miles from the facility, which was one of many reasons the cops didn't buy a word of it.

They all got rounded up and came back only to have extra time added for escaping. There is no who, why or how to explain their logic. I guess inmates aren't to be trusted, which is why they ended up in jail to begin with.

CHAPTER 44

Cherish Every Moment

I often think about how fast life speeds by us. When you're young everything seems to take so long to get to 13. Then driving, graduation, college, marriage, children, 35, 45, 55, 60 and beyond.

I want to be around for my grandchildren and spend time with my great wife. But it seems God has me on a speeding train racing toward his homestead in the sky, high-balling towards the end of a new beginning.

I've seen a lot of people I've known dropping by the wayside, passing on to the afterlife.

Marcia and I have lost our parents, so a little advice: enjoy your parents, your kids and friends. Even though they can be a pain in the ass sometimes, I wish I still had mine around. I miss my mom and dad.

You see yourself getting old, but you need to keep busy and get out and do things. You're only as old as you let yourself be.

Our two grandsons, Jacob and Sam, are now in Florida. We have them for two months and what a joy, but they can tire you out pretty fast.

Marcia keeps saying the kids can do no wrong and she spoils them beyond measure. I guess that's what grandparents are supposed to do.

CHAPTER 45

A Preventable Tragedy

Bucky Phillips was a State inmate being held in the county jail. He worked in the kitchen which was basically unsupervised in the morning. This was because the civilian cook and his supervisor hid in his office.

I'm sorry this event happened at all, but I'm thankful it happened after I retired. Phillips escaped from the Erie County Correctional Facility in 2006.

The cook stayed in the back storage area and the inmates ran the place.

So left unsupervised, Bucky took a large can opener and poked a hole through the ceiling and one of the vent pipes, which led out to the roof.

He should never have been allowed to work there in the first place.

Bucky went on to evade capture for more than five months. He was on the run all summer that year. Oddly, Bucky became a bit of a folk hero, but that viewpoint was way off base.

Bucky was eventually captured, but not before leaving a trail of destruction. One innocent man was killed because State Troopers shot someone they thought was their fugitive.

The situation was tense. Bucky shot at State Troopers in two separate encounters, wounding three troopers, and sadly Trooper Joseph Longobardo lost his life in the line of duty.

Bucky pleaded guilty to aggravated murder and attempted murder charges and was sentenced to life without parole.

The escape was brushed under the table if I recall correctly, but I believe it was actually the Sheriff Department's fault for allowing the escape to happen in the first place.

In the old days you were responsible for things you did and guys were afraid to fuck up. If the kitchen was better guarded, this incident might have been prevented.

Now the guys don't care and everything is done

half-assed because no one is held accountable. You used to get three days leave without pay, fined or fired when you messed up, but that doesn't happen anymore. It's a joke.

CHAPTER 46

Always Be Kind

We used to get a lot of bums in the prison, and I saw a lot of them in Buffalo when I went downtown.

When I saw bums on the streets, I always tried to help them out if they were hustling to make a buck, like sweeping a bar out, collecting beer cans, etc.

I had this one inmate who worked for me in prison. His name was Buffalo Billy and he was about 70 years old. He always had something going on so whenever I got the chance, I always gave him a cigar or a couple bucks, a new ball cap, something.

I never gave out money - or anything - if someone was just begging. I know this sounds harsh, but you must be doing something to earn it.

I can't imagine going through life with nothing or no one. And maybe I have a soft spot for those down and out and less fortunate from all my years working in the prison.

When you get to know people and know their stories, even those that have made enough mistakes to end up in jail, it's hard not to feel compassion for them. I always cheered for them to turn their lives around.

It costs very little to help someone or to be kind to someone. Remember everyone is someone's son, brother or father.

CHAPTER 47

Jimmy "The Saint"

I was home the other day looking through the Buffalo Evening News and I spotted that one of my gang members passed away, Jimmy O'Shea. This guy always had a big Irish smile and a good joke. He always worked for me when he came in.

Marcia and I would run into him bartending in different bars and restaurants around Buffalo. We were at a restaurant near the airport and I was walking to the bathroom. I was in the hallway and I heard someone yelling my name from the lounge.

"Hey Spanky!" shouted Jimmy. "What are you doing here? Get Marcia and come over to the bar and have a drink. It's on me."

Well, drinks were on him and we exchanged stories for two hours.

He told me his brother Billy owned a bar on Washington Street called the Golden Swan and said we should stop in for a drink. So that's just what we did and we came to love the place. The barmaid, Diane, the clients and Jimmy, who had this great-looking girlfriend, Marcia. So when we went out and we met anyone it was Jim and Marcia and Jim and Marcia and everyone thought we were putting them on.

Bow Tie Billy was in love with my wife and loved the perfume she wore, every time we came in, he would want to smell her. He would always say you guys raise the place up when you come in all gussied up.

Billy's patrons were a tough bunch of workers and street people. The place was old, dirty and dingy, but it drew you back. Billy would always light a candle and place it in front of Marcia and me.

He would then start bitching about his brother Jimmy. He drinks too much, he smokes too much and he should stop using drugs. He also thought Jimmy was stealing money out of the cash register when he worked in the bar.

I guess all brothers argue and have disagreements, something you never grow out of I guess.

Jimmy's girlfriend stuck with him no matter what.

It's magical and wonderful when you find someone and they can see the good in you. Everyone needs someone that believes in them unconditionally.

Jimmy always told me that I was the only normal friend he had. We would often go out on the town and always stopped for a night cap at the Golden Swan.

The sad part is Jimmy passed on way too early. He lived the fast life and it took its toll on his body as he was only 53 years old. Jesus must have been looking for a guy to check I.D.s at His door. Well, he got a good man, Jimmy "The Saint" O'Shea.

His brother couldn't get a hold of us because our phone was unlisted, but God had me open the paper just in time to see Jimmy's picture. We then made it to the funeral at the church to say goodbye. I know he is at peace at last.

CHAPTER 48

Setting A Good Example Goes A Long Way

Later on in my career it seemed the new officers were only interested in what was good for them. Getting other officers in trouble by blowing someone in and trying to make themselves look good.

They had no respect for fellow officers and definitely none for the inmates. I know a lot of younger officers could not stand me. They didn't believe that if you gave respect you would get it back in return.

Throughout my 34 years I never changed or falsified a write up. If you were guilty I wrote what happened. Then whatever sentence you received was on you.

I never made calls to get anyone slammed nor did I bitch about the outcome. I wouldn't let this eat me up, but the new COs just felt they could do whatever they wanted. I feel if you are fair and just, you will be judged that way.

Most of the new officers were cowboys. They needed a gun and took what they wanted.

I guess I'm lucky because I believe that you reap what you sowed on the job.

I was always much happier when I found the inmates had had enough and started to do better. In corrections it must start with corrections. We need to set examples and show them the way forward. Looking down on them and swearing or treating them like shit accomplishes nothing. They are human beings.

Now don't get me wrong they were not angels by any means. But we must make the first move. They are going to need a job when they are released, so trying to help them get there I always felt was part of the job.

It seems like we are back to being a big warehouse, where inmates learn nothing and are treated like sheep. When they are released they are no better off than when they entered the prison.

It remains to be seen, but I do not think the system is working for the betterment of the inmates.

CHAPTER 49

Work Hard, Play Scrabble

With any job, you never know what you're gonna get with a new boss.

At a time when we had a new chief giving the orders, it was chaotic. He was a South Buffalo boy and was known to be a drinker.

One day just before I left my shift we had a call in because they thought someone may have escaped. I secured my unit and called a head count into Central Control. After it was over and everything was secured, I was called to the chief's office.

"You were supposed to take these men back to their units," he yelled as he continued to tell me how

I should do my job. "Make sure it doesn't happen again!"

Well, after getting my ass chewed out, I went back and looked in our rule book. It stated that if you're on a work detail you are to keep your men and call in your head count. Not wanting to drop it, I made a copy and went back and showed him.

He didn't know what to say, but he never said he was sorry.

"Oh, well we're going to change that," was his reply.

It was like a Chinese fire drill all the time. No one knew what was going on under this guy's leadership - or lack thereof I should say.

Lt. Dan the Man, who was a mountain of a man (a big son of a bitch), was the only one with common sense. We would play scrabble about three days a week at the end of our day for about 45 minutes. This was while the place was locked down for the change of shift.

We had a lot of fun and looked forward to our battles, even though I won the majority of the games. This man knew how to get things done and how to talk to officers and the inmates.

I never took a break or a lunch for nearly 30 years, so late in my career I took a little down time at the end of my shift to clear my mind, like the little breaks to fit in a game of scrabble.

CHAPTER 50

A Proper Resting Place

Steve Nemith passed away, was cremated and we put his ashes to rest in our grave.

He died because he was a heroin addict. He could never get that monkey off his back. He ended up back in the county jail time and again, and he always gave my name as his next of kin when being processed in.

"Steve, you have to stop doing this because I'll have to bury you someday," I told him.

We always had a good laugh about it.

Marcia and I were on vacation when Steve passed. When we returned home there was a message on my phone to call the Sheriff's investigator. He broke the

I'm sitting (on right in dark shirt) with Steve Nemith (standing behind me on far right) along with other commissary workers.

news, told me what happened to Steve and explained the protocol was that he would be cremated and placed in a common grave.

I just couldn't let that happen. Steve was such a good guy. He deserved more than a common grave!

I talked to Marcia and together we decided we wanted to put him in our grave plot. So we got in touch with an undertaker we knew. He said it would cost around $1,200 to do what had to be done, but he would take care of everything.

The undertaker said he never heard of a correctional officer sharing his grave with an inmate.

You must admit I have a great wife. I can't tell you how much this meant to me.

Steve was like a brother to me. Marcia never hesitated. She just said, "Do it."

CHAPTER 51

A Prayer For Peace

When I started at the prison, we wore light-blue shirts and gray pants with no hats or patches. Then we had the police look, light-blue shirts and gray pants with patches and caps.

When we moved to the new prison, we went to brown uniforms with Stetson hats. We looked like park rangers with patches. Finally, we shifted to the Buffalo Police style. Dark-blue everything, police caps and patches that were changed to Sheriff when the Sheriff's Department took over the prison.

When I first started working the commissary job, I was just the fill in, the relief pitcher until the senior officer retired. I got called into the office and only had five years on the job, but they offered me the full-time job running the commissary.

When I found out the schedule for this job gave me Saturdays and Sundays off, I said, "Sign me up!"

It was a dream come true and we would be like a regular family. I would be home on weekends with Marcia, Dawn and Marlo. I ran the commissary for the next 29 years.

We made up special bags (Goodie Bags) for the inmates who went beyond the call with work. For kitchen help, trustees, library help, commissary help, wherever someone did a good job, I tried to recognize them. It was a little incentive that the inmates called Spanky Bags. I am told they still call them that today.

On my own I also helped inmates who had nothing. I would see they got toothpaste, Oodles of Noodles or some candy bars to help them get over the hump.

I never treated anyone like they were less than me, only as an equal. You would be surprised by the old world respect that's given to you.

After I retired, I worked part time for the county. I audited Senior Centers that feed seniors for $2.25 a meal. There were 47 sites throughout the county, and the funny thing is, all these years later I'd run into inmates who grew old with me. They all wanted to talk about when we were in jail together.

It's really great to hear good things about yourself that you thought people didn't notice.

I wanted people to do what's right, get a job, stay clean and be at home with their family. I wanted inmates to find the good within them and I wanted them to know that change is possible.

The inmates were to blame for why they ended up in jail, but each and every one had the power to change their future. I wanted them to put prison behind them and to move forward on a good path and in a positive direction toward a new life.

I had a long career and worked for a lot of different superintendents during my time as a correctional officer. First it was Mr. Meyers followed by Mr. Mindy. Then came Mr. Ford, who moved on after five months, followed by Mr. Festa.

Then it was Mr. Gallagher followed by Mr. Netzel. Now the Sheriff's Department is in charge of the Erie County Correctional Facility.

It was a great ride.

I learned a lot about people and through it all I always tried to do the right thing.

We live in an imperfect world surrounded by individuals all trying to find their special place. However, we are all aging each and every day as Father Time keeps ticking on and we all will meet our maker in the end.

I sincerely hope and pray everyone reading this can find their quiet place, find peace and have God in the center of their life when it ends.

Afterword

I didn't set out to become a correctional officer, but it was a job I was thankful for and one I never took for granted. I always gave it my all and worked hard to provide for my family.

While it may seem odd that I speak highly of the inmates I was tasked with guarding, it is not weird to me at all. While everyone that ended up in prison did some bad things to justify the punishment, I didn't view myself as above them because I was a guard and they were inmates. We are all human, we all make mistakes and we all deserve second chances.

I treated everyone with dignity and respect as long

as they respected me. And since I had numerous inmates work for me in the commissary over the years, I got to know them and their stories well. I couldn't help but root for them to improve themselves and I always tried to set a positive example so they could see a better way forward.

On the following pages are pictures of some "Gang" members that worked for me in the commissary. Their names are omitted intentionally, but they all worked their way through their prison terms and all worked to improve themselves. Some left and never came back while others rotated back in too often, but I never stopped trying to help and guide them.

Above and on previous page, inmates pose for pictures in the commissary. Below, I'm standing (far right) and sharing a few laughs with the prison staff.

Above, three smiling faces working for me in the commissary. Below, I'm standing behind the counter (second from left) with a few helpers for the day.

Above, I'm standing (far right) and working to keep inventory in order. Below, I'm standing (second from right) with a few hard-working inmates.

Above, I'm standing (middle) with two inmates. Below, this group helped assemble "Spanky Bags" that were awarded to inmates that gave extra effort at work.

About The Author

James Haas is a gifted storyteller and is always quick with a joke. He's a husband, a father, a grandfather, a cherished son and brother, a trusted co-worker and a friend to everyone he has met.

After retiring from a distinguished 34-year career as a correctional officer, Jim dusted off the journals he compiled from his time inside the prison walls and this book is a result of that effort.

Jim's larger-than-life personality, humor, integrity and love for his fellow humans shines through in his stories of the everyday events that happened on the job. The compassion, caring and respect that Jim showed to others, no matter their station in life, is something we can all aspire to match.

Jim is a huge baseball fan and a lifelong New York Yankees fan. Since childhood, he's been an avid sports card collector and is the owner of Spanky's Sports Collectibles. Born and raised in western New York, Jim is a big fan of all Buffalo sports teams: the Bills, the Sabres and the Bisons.

As a Corvette enthusiast, Jim is the proud owner of a sleek red Corvette accessorized with a custom license plate that reads: SPANKY. This ride doubled as his modern day sleigh as he joyfully portrayed Santa Claus every holiday season for many years to spread cheer, hope and laughter to kids.

Jim is a graduate of Maryvale High School and now lives in Lancaster, New York with his wife Marcia and their dog Duchess. This is his first book.

The badge that Jim proudly wore for 34 years working at the Erie County Correctional Facility.

Thank You

Thank you so much for reading this book. It has been a pleasure to share my experiences with you. If you enjoyed this book, please consider leaving a book review on the website where you bought the book.